Choose Joy!

REFLECTIONS ON THE CHOSEN LIFE

Choose Joy!

REFLECTIONS ON THE CHOSEN LIFE

DORI JEANINE SOMERS

ISBN: 978-1-64713-378-8   (Paperback Edition)
ISBN: 978-1-64713-379-5   (Hardcover Edition)
ISBN: 978-1-64713-377-1   (E-book Edition)

Book Ordering Information

Phone Number: 347-901-4929 or 347-901-4920
Email: info@globalsummithouse.com
Global Summit House
www.globalsummithouse.com

Printed in the United States of America

Dedication

*With a tip of my hat, I dedicate this collection
to my intrepid fellow writers—members of the
Coffee House Writers Group Saturday Critique.
I especially honor the poetry disbelievers for
their willingness to listen and learn to love...*

I have chosen the life I live.
It is up to me to decide how I will greet each day,
how I will respond or react to all life brings me.
I choose.
I invite you, with these small offerings,
to join me in celebrating the gift of choice
and the power of positivity.
Look into the mirror of your own inner quiet
and reflect with me on the chosen life.

Contents

SIMPLE PLEASURES

MINISTRY

AGING

COMPANIONS

SNIPPETS

WORDS

CHOICE

Living As If. . .

The way we choose to create our lives often rests on our willingness to "live as if..."

As I gather my thoughts about living "as if," I think of the dandelion and honeysuckle feeding the bees, and remember the title poem in my first book demanding I name them *Weeds? or Wildflowers*! I wrote:

> ...call me the creative realist,
> taking life as it is,
> and designing my own experience
> as it can be. And so I choose
> FLOWERS!

The choice is mine and the message remains that we choose to be positive or negative, and so create the life we live.

Whistle a Happy Tune

In the 1951 musical, *The King and I*, Anna Leonowen, a British gentlewoman, is called to the court of the Siamese king to serve as a teacher for his many wives and children. Far from his home and surrounded by strangers, her small son, Louis, is frightened by the stern-faced counsel to the king, and Anna offers some magnificently wise advice. She sings the song, "Whistle a Happy Tune," comforting her son and herself.

1

"*Whenever I feel afraid,*" Anna sings, admitting her own fears. She then confesses that she pretends to be brave, stands tall, and fools everyone by whistling happily. The happiness she projects with her melody however, doesn't just convince others she is brave, it makes her feel stronger, and convinces her as well. Soon, she tells her son, if you pretend to be brave, *you may be as brave as you make believe you are.* This is the power of living as if. . .

Thinking of the wisdom and power in *living as if,* I heard that simple melody in my head and chased it down on the internet. I printed out the lyrics, and felt a sense of awe that the message was there, on the American theatre stage so many decades ago. Truth, I discovered, is not limited to any particular time; it spans the generations, and wisdom is found in art through the ages.

Choosing...

Every minute each of us is choosing,
Selecting what we'll do and be and say.
Life's co-creators, each on our own pathway
Yet One on the human journey day by day.
Choosing.

Chosen...
Shamen, leaders, mates and priests are chosen
By gift, by love, by calling, or by lot...
To love us—share a life empowered, enriching
That we may live aware of the joy we've got
We've Chosen.

Choose joy!
Spirit of Life is this sweet Joy transcending—
Rising above all sorrow, fear or pain.
Expressed in kindness, breathed in gentle teachings
Like grace, our birthright, gifting us again.
Choose joy

Courage

Pioneer Unaware

This woman is well and truly blessed—gifted with love and living in great abundance. I have been called pioneer, badass, and holy woman, but in a life so full I hardly noticed the extraordinary nature of my ordinary days. Looking back I am aghast, as I recall my place in feminine progress and change.

A pioneer? Me? Well, there were a few things. . .

Girls were not members of the backstage crew or Stagecraft Club in my high school days, but when not emoting on stage I chose to join the male techies and make use of my artistic gifts to enhance the sets. No one but the senior class was allowed on the Yearbook staff, yet I was appointed assistant editor in my junior year. And teenagers were rarely to be found among newspaper reporters or columnists as was I, the kid who wrote a column regularly for the *Mount Holly Herald*.

As a young business woman in fifties Philadelphia, I was among the first non-secretarial females in the banking department of Provident Trust Company, staffing the foreign and collection desk from my seat beneath the famed Millet painting of "The Sowers."

When newly wed, I traveled alone across the Atlantic (off the grid) to Germany, where I joined my non-commissioned husband and lived in a room rented from German town folk. Later, as a young mother, I answered my thespian calling acting in children's theatre, and honed my writing skills as woman's news editor and feature writer for four weekly papers covering towns along the New Jersey banks of the Delaware River.

Ministry was clearly a pioneer path, first as half of an early husband and wife co-ministry team, then as one of only two women among California's Unitarian Universalist Ministers. My dear friend Jon introduced me to Ray Bradbury as the prettiest minister in California— with those odds, not a hard call. Public reaction to a woman serving in ministry made it clear I trod a path not often braved by women. And so it was. Or so I was—a pioneer, unaware.

The next poem honors June Somers-Cook, purveyor of smiles and applause, and her siblings' art of theatre which she so admired and encouraged. Writing it when the demon cancer stole her from us was my act of healing and courage.

The origins of the theatrical expression "break a leg" may rest in Shakespearian times when it served as a description for the artist's bow to bend (or break) the leg. Professor Ed Wright encouraged his Dennison University actors, however, to

Light up the space!

Light up the space!

In theatre lore they tell us
"Good luck" must not be said,
So thespians encourage friends
With "break a leg" instead.

The maestro knows, however,
Of the power of a smile
As it becomes a beacon
To enchant and to beguile.

He knows this craft is more than luck.
It's skill and work and choice,
And sending forth the writer's truth.
And so he lifts his voice…

Inspiring the actor's art—
Life, energy and grace
Igniting incandescence
As he calls, "Light up the space!"

Wisdom of the Trees

Listen to the trees, hear them whisper and sing. Or if your ears betray you and hide that arboreal conversation, notice instead the images before your eyes—the exquisite filigree and lacy array of leaves, slender shoots and sprays of green, near green, gray, brown, or yellow the eye may register. What do you learn from the trees? What precious secrets do they tell you? What gifts do they offer?

I sat on my patio and breathed in the fragrant breeze, appreciating the beauty of the foliage so generously arrayed across the cement block wall, that sun-warmed playground so beloved by swift-footed little lizards performing their silent happy dance.

One gift of beauty found on that patio and in the verdant fringes of our yard is the array of shades and textures, shapes and sizes in the many plants, shrubs, and trees that bless us. That master artist—God, nature, or the cosmos—has captured simplicity, complexity and variety in shades of green. And I wonder what I am to learn from all this exquisitely subtle beauty.

Reaching into the treasure box of adjectives the scene has inspired, I take my lesson from the very words I have chosen to describe it—*simplicity, complexity, variety*—then extend the gift to include *gratitude.* I am thankful. I give thanks for the simple beauty of the earth, the amazing array of differences in my variegated greening garden, the complicated and miraculous reality of growing things, and of myself and you, and I find courage day by day.

Bravely Plant Bulbs

I have read that planting bulbs is courageous, an act of faith. Picture those brown lumps a gardener sticks into the ground each fall expecting an array of flowers come spring. Sometimes the flowers don't arrive, the bulbs may be eaten by animals or shriveled in the winter's cold. But more often they do indeed bloom and even multiply underground, blessing us with more than we ever hoped to see.

In much the same way, faith in ourselves brings forth sometimes unexpected gifts. Our expectations are regularly met and often exceeded as we create our reality with the power of thought and conviction. So I plant bulbs of beauty in my daily life that they may multiply and surround me with tranquility, energy and delight.

My Song
A bird doesn't sing
because it has an answer,
it sings because it has a song.
    Maya Angelou

And what is my song? For lo these many years it has been a melody of hope and possibility, a courageous happy tune whistled in the dark corners of life to reassure me of my own bravery and my belief in the good. Mine is a song of joy and laughter, optimism and beauty, gratitude and generosity, forgiveness and love.

To sing one's song when no one is listening is not easy, but perhaps it is not necessary to be heard, but only to free the music and bathe myself in the meaning and the melody. If my song is my heart's message and my strength comes from the passion within me, I am the one who must listen to the song.

The Color Orange
Bright orange, a writers' prompt reminds me, is a bold statement and stands out from the crowd. Indeed.

That particular assessment reminds me of the Diane von Furstenberg inspired wrap dress I'd tucked into my closet in 1974 Bangor, Maine. I'd never cared much for the color orange, but this was what was available at an affordable price. I might not ever wear it.

The dress was waiting for me, however, on that horrible Sunday morning when my husband and co-minister left and moved into the home of his lover. I was scheduled to preach and I would not tremble and hide. I gathered my inner forces and donned the orange dress. In that time of challenge it became a shield and a dramatic statement, my red badge of courage.

I still harbor mixed feelings about the color orange, shunning the garden's offerings of Marigold and Cana, but I delight in the softer hues of the orange spectrum—pale amber, melon, peach. I play with exotic combinations using burgundy or leafy green to create something lovely. And I even choose to stand out from time to time in outrageous orange.

* New attitude—two years later. I have been charmed by a chorus line of perky Cana gifted me by a friend. Those orange ladies delight me!

we persisted

at eighty-six, I struggled to continue
the unending uphill climb toward justice
one step at a time...

yet some have accused me
of being an accomplice
in all that is wrong today—
oppressive, racist, inhumane
behaviors and evil systems—
my very faith called out as an enemy
steeped in mistaken tradition.

some of us have lived
with these evils and fought them
for seventy-five years
or more...
one tiny step at a time.
does that not matter?
did no one notice?

does no one remember
our determination to give women
dominion over their own lives?
our demands to allow those who love to marry?
the struggles to support persons of color,
those in need of sanctuary?

today's battles are fought today
but we whom you denounce
built the barricades
on which you stand
and passed down our own small
victories amid the ruins

born into a culture
of white male supremacy
misogyny and greed
we could do only what we could do
to make a difference...
and we persisted.

The Advent season was upon us, and we were unprepared, as good folks are unprepared for inhuman, evil acts of violence. Unprepared for another shooting, this time in nearby San Bernardino. What to do? How do I greet the holiday season amid the heartbreak?

with no apology
the guns of evil have rained destruction
and I greet strangers at our door
with gentle smiles...
for someone must.

tragedy fills the ears and minds of everyone.
I decorate—create beauty
in honor of the holy season
celebrated in light...
for someone must.

anger blooms into rage
and anguish moves toward despair,
yet I encourage laughter,
treasure gifts of smiles
and songs of praise...
for someone must.

the wicked spew out hatred fear and lies,
manipulate the news and feed their greed.
and I continue writing words of love
depicting beauty here amid the blood...
for someone must.

God weeps as I must weep
still singing of the blessed gifts
of grace and joy...
for someone must
someone must
someone
surely
must

Kneeling before the flag

FOOLS, KNAVES, IDIOTS!
Have you never been within the walls
of any church or house of worship?
Are you so blind you do not see
the truth behind the bended knee?

Within communities of faith
the people stand to sing,
and to rejoice and press the hand of peace.
The faithful kneel...
to pray.

Prayers arise and carry unto God
our pain, our fears,
our deepest yearning for the good.
Upon our knees do we confess our sins
and speak to God of joy and sorrows.

Yet no one speaks about the giant lie
broadcast by those who call it disrespect
to "take the knee,"
when it's so wrong to stand
and celebrate the evils done

in our name, by our kin—
by those who've shattered our respect
with cruel disregard
for those they label "other".
Kneel sister. Kneel brother.

There is nothing more respectful.

Sweetness
(inspired by the sweet face
of Jesus in "Godspell")

In this world plagued with bitter realities
Life is enriched by the faces so sweet
The flavor of honey in words of affection
The smile of a friend or a stranger I meet.

You are so sweet, I have said to my puppy
Knowing his mission in life is to be
A living reminder of God's unconditional
Love—perfect, endless, for you and for me.

While the cynic calls saccharine all that is gentle
And laughs in his bitterness, thinking me weak
I can rejoice still and savor the sweetness
Remembering blessings bestowed on the meek.

GRATITUDE

To Give Thanks
Sweet are the uses of adversity,
Which, like the toad, ugly and venomous,
Wears yet a precious jewel in his head;
And this our life exempt from public haunt
Finds tongues in trees, books in the running brooks,
Sermons in stones and good in every thing.
I would not change it.
    Duke Senior from "As You Like It"
      William Shakespeare

Is adversity indeed so useful? Is it adorned like Shakespeare's toad, with a precious jewel? Does it carry wisdom so rich that we can discover messages in the brooks and trees, sermons in the very stones?

Throughout the years I have taught that our dark moments blossom into joy-filled light, that sorrows are laden with gifts and lessons. Before ever encountering this example of the Bard's wisdom I knew these truths, and shared them. In my second poetry collection I included a poem blessing my burdens and crises, and called it **For Hidden Gifts**

Every prayer a thanksgiving
Every poem a prayer
In burdens, quiet blessings
In darkness, love and care.

Each shadow brings new insight
New gentleness or friends.
Each crisis brings a hidden gift
And sacred joy transcends.
Every prayer a thanksgiving
Every poem a prayer
As kindness grows within the heart
And beauty blossoms there.

Let this be my prayer of thanks each day as I celebrate life's treasures.

in gratitude for
An Ordinary Life

mine is an ordinary life
as all our lives must seem
extraordinary in its gifts
and in life's glorious scheme
this shared and treasured life

there may be threats or fear, or pain
there may be sorrow too
but I have lessons to be learned
and caring acts to do
in this courageous life

my laughter fills the emptiness
with humor, wit and spark
permitting bold mischievousness
to brighten up the dark
in this outrageous life

the children gather to be held
and fed and nurtured well
each loved and learning, listening
to stories that we tell
in this parental life

the blessings that have come to us
the joys that we have known
wear friends' and family's faces
proving we are not alone
in this remembered life

each moment carries beauty
each action holds a sign
of promise and of poetry
reflecting life's design
in this creative life
this precious life, this noble life
this life of yours and mine

sing hallelujah

as I address
the universe
in prayer
this is the simple message
I declare...
I am thankful.

images of joy spill in my mind
remembered laughter
of the gulls so fine
tang of salt air, and
music of the waves
like waters that my childhood
memory saves
and I would wish to sing—
sing hallelujah

rejoice, give thanks,
and sing—
sing hallelujah

joy bubbles up
as from a woodland spring
sing hallelujah
as gratitude pours forth
in mighty streams
hallelujah
sing hallelujah

I ride upon the waves
white waters rage
and murmur thanks
for all the beauty
of life's gifts
oh, hallelujah

tho shadows lurk
upon the banks
beckoning, to show me
hate and sorrow
I choose to be creator
of the good
sing hallelujah

by strength of thought
to make it rise
and shout life's glory
to the skies
sing hallelujah

gainsay the path
cluttered and bleak
lest I create
all that I'd hate
sing hallelujah
sing hallelujah
that with thanks
and joyful presence

heaven grants
for evermore
her gifts of beauty
hallelujah

In Quietness.
September 29, 1997 - Serra Retreat Center

To give thanks...
      To rejoice...
To know again the silent song of peace...
Truths sighing on the breeze
      that sent me home.
Here Spirit is...
      as God is...
      everywhere.
Yet *here*
      the heart responds
      and thought takes flight,
And *knowing*
      is the gift
      in quietness.

A Mother's Gratitude

lucky mother? lucky child?
or is it all about the timing?
much has changed

gratitude engulfs me
feeling blessed by
all you've been and are—
my children.

no demand to understand, no
bazaar behaviors, anguished needs.
you flourished.

when I view the generation
now before us all so different
in their living

new demands for blind acceptance
leave me grieving for a normal
undefined.

never having faced these pitfalls
I am thankful for my daughters
and my son.

With Thanks to MAYA

for Maya, angel, goddess, muse,
master poet of an age
hers the words that lit the soul
she it was who set the stage.

writing, singing, bringing truth
we who follow stir the mind
she has taught us *we shall rise*
love is spoken by our kind

what is your kind they ask and frown
and with that question limit light
upon the path, and fail to see
the grander images of right

our kind changes destiny
ours the saviors of the earth
writing poems and telling truths
sharing what the planet's worth

our kind, humankind indeed
womankind and all who care
genders more than simply two
live our truth with love to spare

colorful or colorless,
young or old, renown or shy,
speaking with the voice of life
our kind's songs will never die.

Life is rich. So much to learn, so much to live for.

Life Is...

Life is good. I posted this upon my desktop.
Life is wild. I watch the circus passing, non-stop.
Life is rich. So much to learn, so much to live for,
So many friends to meet, so much to give for.
Life is fun. The days and nights alight with laughter.
Life is hopeful. Joy is ours "forever after."
Life is sad, but we have learned to find the lesson,
The gift of light in darkness, and the blessing.
Life is ours to celebrate, appreciate and sing of.
My wish for you—
      may each day shine with joy and bring love.

A Grace for Thanksgiving

Give thanks
for eyes and ears, fingers and toes
for clear water and fresh air
for breath

Give thanks for family and friends
For bright moments of laughter,
and tender hands that dry our tears
For hearts mended and medical miracles
for doctors and nurses, teachers, farmers
and factory workers, poets and singers of songs

Give thanks for simple acts of kindness
generosity, hospitality and welcome
for all things bright and beautiful;
for trees...
for dogs and cats,
elephants and otters
For moonlight on the mountains
and sunlight on the seas

We give thanks
We give thanks
We give thanks

HOME

Serene Souls

Where there's heart room, there's house room.
I may not have told you this in the book, *Serenity*. Another easy source
of peace and serenity you can tap is the presence of a serene soul. Their
tranquility is healing. Our pets are aware of this simple gift, and happily
settle themselves beside quiet, gentle persons—those whom we might
call mellow. Children and teens often prefer the space where such folks
have surrounded themselves with quiet beauty. You too will find house
room in those places, as serene souls are welcoming people with lots of
heart room. Come in, dear friends, come in!

Making a Home

Like homesick snails we're unaware
that home is heartroom we can share
with loved ones... gather, touch and tend
guide and nurture, host a friend.
With our presence beauty blooms
in pillows, flowers, books and rooms
warmed and brightened by our care
we take home with us everywhere

And so it is.

My Parlor

There is, at the tip of my toes, a "fireplace" dancing with flames so real they make me worry lest my little feet should be singed. This technically created illusion comforts and soothes me, and on cold mornings the accompanying heater actually removes the chill. My cottage is so much more than a converted garage; it is a dream home.

The Door to Bestemor Cottage
Bestemor - Grandma in Norwegian

I rest facing the undraped picture window with my front door flung wide, and gaze upon an ancient oak, a great and graceful pine. The tangled and blackened framework of a pear tree, long dead, and yellow blooms on flowering bushes tuck themselves into the frame formed by the window's edge. And I am moved to share poetry.

The Glow of Delight

a home awaits discovery
a nest, a haven, a retreat
a place of rest that shelters love
all orderly and neat.
how little space it seems to take
for quiet to ignite
the simple walls and table tops
with glow of sheer delight.
here beauty is simplicity
as peace its songs employ
allowing hearts to celebrate
and dance both pain and joy.

Never merely decor
the treasures we keep carry more—
telling where we have been, who we are,
storied memories near and afar.
They are life's

Artifacts—may be how our life's tale is taught.

artifacts

poet...
tell me the stories of things
the Tibetan rice bowl that sings,
the coffeepot marked with a date
from Norway, eighteen sixty eight?
photo of Dad with a hat
(what is more handsome than that?)
or that cute little toddler ('twas you!)
the buddha the child made (it's true)
picture books shared through the years
some sweet ones that brought you to tears
on the lamp a small Hardanger stitchery
on the walls lovely art by the family
etching and sketching and hue,
Grandma's painting of Paris so true,
a mirror quite ancient and grand
with rich royal flags of the land
of your grandparents' parents and line
with Viking face hidden behind.
though "things" are not what we have sought

or coveted, yearned for or bought
the stories they bring and the songs that they sing
may be how our life's tale is taught

Holiday Village
In December, my wee Christmas village sits on the mantle of my mini
fireplace—its brilliant imitation of burning logs tricking the eye, and
the heater warming us (the fur babies and me) whenever the cottage
demands it. As I gaze at the lovely little tableau, it becomes clear that
this is once more, as in all that I design or create, a representation of
my values, my teaching, my very identity, and my wishes for all the
world.

Homes are here, places of love, of safety and support, and a church
meetinghouse with its sign proclaiming, "Everyone Welcome." There is
a theatre of course, and a quaint shop carrying simple treasures. There
are children at play, and a merry-go-round. A gazebo graces the park
and not far from the gazebo a couple stands with hands clasped as the
tiny white-haired minister—clearly identifiable as Rev. Dori—blesses
their marriage. In one corner there are trees gifting us with oxygen
and in the other corner, a lighthouse guarding the people and sending
forth the light of love and reason. Above it all, joyous flowers bloom,
their red blossoms reminding us of all there is to bless us in the season
of light and love.

Keeping Cool in Summer
for comfort my cooling is subtle
the view from my window of trees
all dancing a windy fandango
reminds me of wintery breeze.

the photo I chose for my laptop
the backdrop for all that I read
is surf as it splashes and crashes
on rocks with the crisp cool we need

but here at the foot of the mountain
in a place called the inland empire
our sweet cultured city is roasted
in temperatures crafted like fire

so the brilliance of imagination
and a workplace in front of a fan
lend a touch of the coolness we're seeking
in the mind when not in nature's plan

SOLITUDE

Solitude

solitude . . . so sweet
when carried on the breeze
and hosted by the birds
alone and not alone
amid the small dogs' songs
and whirring fans' imagined words

a door stands open
calling welcome to a world
uncluttered with remorse and full of light
then joy walks in
not needing to announce
the gifts of grace that bless us day and night

Time on my hands
Use active voice. I take more time (actively, of course) to write than once
I did. No more dashed off first drafts, no perfectly imperfect poems
shuttled along to my well-read offspring. Today I write and rewrite,
correct and polish, search for that exquisitely perfect word, certain it
must await me. . . somewhere. It takes time.

And time is my wealth and my gift. I have an abundance of quiet moments and hours, with only myself to please, only the dogs for company, only the muse to serve. I can simply write—"militantly positive" poetry or prose. I close my eyes and listen to the music within, discover some new thought, and give thanks for the joy that abounds.

Solitude so sweet...

the symphony of silence

in the concert hall named "quietness"
bright notes of wind chimes sound
a distant choir is voiced by dogs
and songs of birds abound

the whirring of a ceiling fan
that whispers through the night
accompanies the neighbor's car
and growling planes in flight

an auto horn disturbs the calm
the whistle of a train
recalls me to the wider world
and all I have to gain

out there beyond the boisterous
silence I've enjoyed alone
where solitude creates a path
to peace, and joy is known

Never Bored

Happily, boredom has not been a problem for me. My interior landscape
is so exciting and rich with color and activity that I find interest,
challenge, and entertainment there among the thoughts, the images of
yesterday and plans for tomorrow.

A posting for spiritual practice asks the question, *"How does your
imagination lead you into magic?"* And this seems an appropriate sidebar
to my comment on my fortunate state of non-boredom. An aware and
awake approach to life seems almost magical in a world where people
have become blasé and jaded, demanding more and more excitement.

People, who constitute "the public," yearn to be stimulated and
entertained. Even the food served in most restaurants seems to cater
to bored appetites with the ubiquitous spiciness of hot peppers. Nudity
and near nudity replaces class and subtle sophistication. Four letter
words replace wit and innuendo. Technological devices stifle face-to-
face interaction and conversation. Magic is needed!

My magic is simple and benign. I write poems and essays, decorate
rooms, invent new uses for old belongings, and decide what I will
give away—keeping myself busy, interested and involved in life.
Solitary thankfulness, creativity and conscious awareness of the beauty
surrounding me enriches my spirit and fills the empty spaces in my
day or evening. Stories and laughter with genuine interest in others
brightens my life with interactions when I am not alone. I am connected
either way. Never bored!

WRITING

About My (Google?) Search
Why would anyone be interested?

But if they were?

I might regale them with tales of my more lackadaisical, useless mental escapades—when wide awake at three in the morning. I might tell them what trivia fills my thoughts or what it is that sends me in search of new truths at strange and unusual hours.

I might confess that sometimes poems haunt me in the night and refuse to follow me into the searing light of day, or that my muse has declared a holiday and refused to whisper in my ear or sing to me in metered beauty as she oft is wont to do.

And then I would announce that a new discovery has brought me hope—this simple so-called prose is in fact the poetry of my soul. And the muse is with me still, even hidden in a commentary or an essay, seeking joy. The Muse and I will create a message of blessing.

prose as poetry—

even when not crafted as a poem
the melody, the harmony and pace
of poetry surrounds the words of prose
enhancing all with a poetic grace

the ears and eyes of those who care the most
are tuned to see and hear the subtle tone
of lilt and language, hidden songs and dreams
depicting life as dance, and joys we've known

the story, lyrical and meaningful
brings thoughts that soar, lets peace and beauty grow
metered words like swelling symphonies
lift the heart and make the spirit glow

magic abides, the spawn of love and fire
the passion of a writer ever true
enamored with the miracle of words
bringing a beauty born of thought made new

poetry...all life is poetry
let the lyrics shine, the music ring
your story too, will be an epic poem
that calls forth everyone to come and sing

and though you name this tale a blog or bit,
a ramble perhaps, or essay—simply prose
deep in the hearts of all who feel the words
there sings a song from which the thought arose

Ocular Fiction

I confess over and over that my wordsmith skills do not run to writing fiction. I don't make up stories, I say—although I can embroider, enhance, or craft a tale to my own liking. I can polish the syntax, add details, strengthen the plot. But I don't invent or bake my story from scratch. I assumed this reflected a certain lack of imagination or creative quirkiness. A drab mindset, perhaps.

Lately, however, I have experienced an interior entertainment that belies that assumption. Being anything but drab, I have developed an unusual kind of unreality (or fiction?) that displays behind my eyes. As I lay awake in my bed some nights my inner movie screen lights up with pictures that have no connection to my conscious thoughts, images that may resemble cartoons or pencil drawings, full color pictures or bland sketches. And these images morph into other images, faster than I can register their details or name them.

I am entertained.

Sometimes I smile (from behind closed eyes) with delight. I may gaze with amazement, curiosity or stunned silence watching a face suddenly acquire glasses, a hairstyle change to one with bangs, a knight swiftly immerge shielded with armor and a helmet. Who is that round faced fellow in the lavender shirt, the gray three-piece suit? I don't recognize the people in these scenarios nor the places the morphing trees, machines and buildings might be found. They are dream stuff, living in my mind's pre-dreaming, pre-sleeping wilderness. And I have created *ocular fiction*.

the mask of make-believe
A writer struggles to be heard
or read, and understood,
avoiding at all costs the dread cliché.
We ignore the fact that a cliché
exists only because it may have
proven through the years,
the best way to "say it".
SO Although....
Truth is (indeed) stranger than fiction
I believe I must not
use that trusted phrase
but write about this truth
in a new and different way.
(I'll try!)

when life has donned the mask of make-believe
surprising us with plot twists and mad turns
we are not sure if we should laugh or disbelieve
and hunger for the truth within us burns

a half forgotten tale of one beloved so long
a story of betrayal and of pain
behavior too bizarre, or too dramatic,
a shocking denouement, what do we gain?

our true life story has been drenched in tears
that drown us 'mid the laughter and the fun
and weird surprises somehow always spiced the years
and set us wond'ring how it had begun

to love someone then learn you never knew him
to give your heart and not regret the cost
to still be truly deeply thankful to him
and know you've gained more than you ever lost

let our story entertain, enlighten
give a shout of joy for gifts received
it doesn't matter if the plot's not tightened
non fiction here is meant to be believed.

The Land of Lost Words

A wordsmith finds joy in collecting words, so I begin this little romp with a collection of terms for what I'm creating here. It might be called an article, treatise, item, write-up, piece, blurb, commentary, discourse, or a feature. And now we add the unlovely sobriquet, *Blog*! I, however, will name it a *reflection*. Whatever it may be called, it's fun for me, and I hope it is for the reader, as well.

Even as I delight in finding exciting and interesting words or enriching a piece with thoughtful phrasing, I hate to lose a word. With a head crammed full of vocabulary, jargon, vernacular, idiom, lexicon, lingo, or nomenclature, I feel immense frustration when the appropriate word fails me. That *just right* word lurks in the shadows of my awareness, taunting me with the conviction that I have known the perfect term for this—whatever it may be. Where is that appropriate label, that perfect term?

I have often wondered and questioned just what happens to lost words. Where do they go? I ponder and conjecture—do they perhaps hide in some *verbacious Neverland* where they make up stories about us, the careless caretakers of language who call ourselves writers?

Wouldn't it be a lark to visit *the land of lost words*? Here we'll find the exact descriptions, compliments, and grammatical perfections that have alluded us from time to time for years. Here we'll note the differing meanings of egoist and egotist (An egotist thinks highly of himself, an egoist thinks only of himself.) Here we are reminded *a cappella* is two words, a *privilege* is a right that may be extended to a group or a number of people; a *prerogative* is a right that, customarily, is vested in a single person—a birthright, an entitlement.

I keep for myself a nerdy little version of the land of lost words in a file titled simply "Memory." Noting how certain words, celebrity names, book titles, plants and animals or concepts repeatedly lose themselves, I decided to create a place where I can quickly retrieve the most likely absconders. Rereading that list of mine is highly entertaining. And sometimes it's fairly enlightening. (In case you'd wondered where the term *perks* originates, it is short for the formal term *perquisites:* fringe benefits, advantage, bonus.)

I am so happy in the land of lost words, I'm somewhat unwilling to leave, but other delights beckon. So I shall return to my reading where I may even find a few new treasures for my word collection. That would delight me.

too little or too much?

I asked myself once in a poem
if I had ceased to harbor thought
and did not ponder as before
the wonders that the day had brought.

was this the reason songs were stilled
the Muse's gifts forfeit or lost. . .
too little thought? no. it was clear
my overthinking had its cost.

in quietness the tranquil mind
would sing. now noisy life has spilled
out so much thinking, worldly woes
that leave the poet unfulfilled.

*Still I refuse to rant. It is not my prerogative to be always artistically
fulfilled. Nor shall I chastise myself for falling short of my best (or even my
better) work. It is true that too much thinking tends to stifle my creative
endeavors, and I would prefer to create. And so I strive to quiet my mind,
reaching for tranquility.*

poems as power

poetry, like fire must be
a source and conduit of power
capturing and heightening
the firm command of truth
exchanging solemn fears for wings,
condensing wisdom often spurned
intensifying, simplifying,
teaching love to age and youth

the poet speaks for each of us
with fewer words and keener sight
truth enhanced, grown swift and strong
meanings more flavorful, more deep
taste the words, enjoy the gift
seasoned with humor, wisdom, grace
open the windows of the soul
these are the songs our hearts must keep

more than music, more than rhyme,
poems carry seeds of change
memories of older grace
for the living of this hour
to become what best you may,
to regain what has been lost
follow the poets' daring songs,
let them be your key to power

The Pen Is Mightier. . .

Years pile up and change is constant. Watching my disappearance as
that early pilgrim with a bold ministry of peace, positivity and universal
kindness, I sometimes shudder at the mirror's image and feel shame lest
I have failed in my mission. No longer do I "walk the walk" of social
justice. I do not mount the barricades in defense of the good for I am
no longer young and nimble.

So I write. I sing of something better, occupy myself with the search
for beauty, laughter, and wisdom. I tell the story of life's gifts, offering
hope. My new friend assures me it is enough.

She hears me calling to the workers still in the fields of struggle,
trembling and weary with the hopelessness of it. She, too is weary and
disheartened. But as she reads or hears my poetry she stands a little
taller—lifted, encouraged, renewed. And so perhaps the barricades can
grow strong without my once sturdy body, defended and invigorated
today by my words.

Obfuscation

Who ever told you it was smart
to hide behind a plethora of words
to speak of things that all of us have heard
in ways sure to confuse and stupefy

Who ever told you it was cool
to darken truth with complicated turns
to make opaque each new thing that you learn
so others although bright won't understand

Who ever told you intellect
was something you should use to stand alone
hiding the meanings we have always known
to claim them for yourself officiously

Who ever told you to becloud
to baffle and befuddle, complicate
conceal, confound, in short to obfuscate
when clarity is simple, short and sweet.

The View from My Window

My first gig as a columnist was for several weekly newspapers in New Jersey. I named my column "The View from My Window."

So many years have gone by, and I have no real memories of that endeavor, except for assurance that the vignettes were pleasant—positive surely. Small town America in the sixties offered an array of topics worthy of Norman Rockwell. And I believe, indeed I hope those images of school and home, garden party, dance, or play, family picnic, clam bake or ski run continue to thrive today—somewhere.

Unfortunately, much of what I have seen in news or social media is violent, hate-filled or alarmist. There are often opinionated rants I would prefer to avoid. And so my challenge is the same as it has been through the years—to tell of life's gifts, its beauty and warmth, of friendship and kindly actions; to share the positive view from my window.

Making Poetry

On Poetry

Poetry—a mating ritual for words
romancing, dancing, soaring high like birds

or making pictures, teaching, healing
bringing peace and deeper feeling

passions spoken, love revealed
covenants expressed and sealed

playful words with colors bright
or sad and tragic truths we write.

and still remind the sad of heart
beauty is theirs to impart

pax vobiscum

for this too
is surely poetry
this peaceful stillness
filling me with joy

furred companions rest
and tall fans sing
as leaves of green and wine
reach for the sun

alone and not alone
held by the thread
that binds, unites all creatures
large and small

and guides me too
keeps loneliness away
and frees within me
songs inspired and true

so many gifts
reside in quietness
so many blessings
hide in open sight

they bid me sing
or share in written word
the treasures I have found
in solitude

Thought Power - *I lay in bed and composed a polite but snarky piece in my head, not ever to be published or posted, voicing my annoyance at some small pet peeve. And I suddenly realized how toxic were these efforts, and how sadly they would fail me, bringing out nothing of my better self. Here is what I learned:*

Thought Power - the poem

thoughts are building blocks,
the Lego pieces of the soul
shaping us, creating us
in their own image.
as I think, so shall I be.

beware, poet.
forego the rants and ravings
for even small complaints
have power to change us
diminish our better selves
and stain our hearts.

celebrate, instead, with songs of joy
and prayers that say a simple
thank you...thank you universe,
thank you, indwelling good,
sweet source of love,
of peace and understanding.

A Poet Writes

Even haters of poetry are surprised and sometimes charmed by discovering a poet who avoids the esoteric in favor of simplicity, melody, and grace. Well-written poems generate amid the ordinary, and reflect the deeply personal yet universal human experience. It is the readers' recognition of themselves within the words that gives a poem life as literature. When the message is hope and beauty, the meaning is never veiled, and the words flow easily, unforced. The result is enjoyable, even to those who have foresworn all liking for the poet's gifts.

Poetry is . . . energy, in metered economies of words.
True poets practice brevity, restraint;
Forgoing self-important adjectives,
Excessive ego, flowery flourishes.
The wise have learned simplicity alone
Ennobles truth, gives meaning clarity,
Lets beauty be not wasted or ignored.
Your favorite songs begin as poetry.
(And you thought you hated that stuff!
* *A poet writes* (not always beautifully) because they cannot refuse to write. I write because I can't not write... and yes, the double negative IS positive, even if the resultant melody is not. And so I am called to

be a poet, winged with words, God's spy, charged with speaking the ordinary with extraordinary precision and clarity. May it be so.

Beauty still reigns, truth is constant.

after a writer's dry spell

'tis a terrible thing for a writer—
weighted by so many years
awaiting the sphere's to bring music
but meeting just silence or tears

what has become of the challenge
where is the pathway so fair
who has the gifts of the cosmos
or truths she's unable to share

poet...
oh, poet! where are you?
what has enticed you away?
have you been lost or abandoned—
muse sad, unwilling to play?

beauty still reigns, truth is constant
why <u>have</u> you not found cause for joy?
a reason to sing of life's treasures
or wisdom your songs can employ

the stories of good do outweigh all
the evil we see in the news
and allow you to answer your calling
to share love in words that you choose

although it's not simple nor easy
making art in the midst of the gale
remember that this is your mission
to help truth and beauty prevail

welcome back, poet!
Birth of a Poem
   through me, not from me

abiding in the Oversoul I listen
and softly sway to music of the spheres
this humble poet, reaching for connection
and holy songs to echo through the years

melody arrives airborne and ringing
in the yearning writer's inner ear,
in tingling fingers on a pen or keyboard,
the whispers of her heart becoming clear

a poem will be born and grown and nurtured
sent forth because the poet spreads the song
played on her soul by something far beyond her
divine assurance that we all belong

tis not of me the poet mildly murmurs
meaning the gift of love she knows so well
songs infinite and sweet and universal
found on the page, when ere there's truths to tell

heaven's scribe...

they named me poet—
thought my gift was strong
tho I am truly merely heaven's scribe
presenting to the world a hopeful song,
a melody of truth, meant to survive.

a simple scribe who writes the words she hears
whenever life might choose to gift her ears
with messages of courage, beauty, light...
and positives inspiring delight.

when quiet creeps upon her fertile mind
and songs of peace and love are hard to find
she listens deeply, hopefully to place
within her heart the poetry of grace.

for surely gracious life has something left
to teach and save the hopeless and bereft.
I pray the universe will give
this faithful scribe the songs we need to live.

may it be so

When a poem, like a puppy, follows me home and I know I must keep it, the little thing may need some grooming. And so yesterday's writing looks a bit different today. (Even better, I hope.)

growth of a poem

in time a poem grows richer, sweeter,
freed to dance and find its meter

changing when a broader view
brings more wisdom than we knew

gained when listeners are moved
to find within some deeper truth

hidden perhaps in melody
sacred joys may be set free

gifts surprising, passions true
even as all life grows new

from the start we take it slow
let the melody just flow

gently ponder how it sings
where it leads and what it brings

send the thought into the sky
listen to the muse reply

as beauty finds another way
and changes pathways day by day

Words on Yellow Legal Pads

does the simple old refrain
rest best in ink on yellow pad
when the hand must glide and bend
to make a true connection?

or is the glint of cyber light
enough to welcome new creation
tapping keys with thumbs or fingers
hoping that the magic lingers

Poet's dilemma

a strange phenomenon—
to be blocked from writing
by the writing in my head,
in my bed
feeling unable to write
because I "wrote"
in the night
without light
unrecorded
unremembered
never visible on a page
but so sage
and crisp
that wisp
of genius
never again to light
my thinking
and I find myself
yearning to recall
words once fired
now uninspired
slow and tired
mind too dull
and empty

A Path to Creativity

take some raw reality
view kaleidoscopically
let angled mirrors
change the shape
and set the limits free

this rearranging of the real
is how the artist grows.
designer, poet, actor, clown
creating as she goes.

look upon me in my home
within your gaze—or all alone
it matters to me not at all—
as I have work to do.

so I shall make
the best of things
with cushions
boards and ribbon strings
to ease, improve, facilitate–
all through.

by using things
for what they're not
intended to be taken for
I make a lot
of comfort or
convenience any day.

this kind of thinking
is the key
to worlds of creativity;
a sidewise view
allows the muse to play.

The Immediacy of Poetry

Here…
Now…
    intensified in words
    that carry joy
or pain
or yearning

    fragrances and
    pictures for the mind
    stories lived and told
    in metered rhyme
Now...
Here...
    the poet breathes and wonders
    what is true
    old wisdom clarifies
    and shines anew
for love
or learning

Lament for Poems Lost
    12/21/08

scraps of paper
shredded notes
faded ink on yellow legal pads
three-ring binders overflow
the ever-shrinking shelves
and must be sent away

the ancient news sheets
literary magazines
gone
all gone
and poems lost
forever

where is the prayer that built a bridge
and earned the critic's praise
united opposites
in spirit one

where is the tribute
to a long lost friend
the love song
sans music
sans rhyming

words once treasured
creep into the mind
in tiny bursts of metered rhyme
sighing
urging...
"remember"

try again
capture the thought
follow the path once trod
and now grown over
like wilderness
all leafy

> *Daily from the mirrored depths*
> *Of the ancient looking glass*
> *A shadowed Viking wise and bold*
> *Watches the lady pass*

what was the rest
how did it flow
what wisdom did it hold

> *And sees the busy mother*
> *Who never seems to know*
> *The beauty in her oval face*
> *Is a modern cameo*

the poems were better then
where did they go
when there were only
words on paper

Poetry contest

How do you measure joy or pain
or love perhaps
or wisdom?
Upon a scale of one to ten
the doctors say.
And then again
the pundits and the judges try
to rank a poem
in worldly competition.

How can one dream be better than?
How can they give a prize?
Say one is best
and leave the rest
unloved
and unrewarded.

The poet's words are poet's flesh
and blood, the fruit of nurture.
Not to be priced
or weighed against—
sent forth to earn a bonus.

We will not compete,
my poems and I.

An Ode To Beauty—

The poet sleeps as beauty blooms
to fill her dreams with light
reminding her of beauty's gifts
and bringing joys so bright

a different way to view the world
the gift of holy grace
to be at last fully aware
of beauty's lovely face

art's fine creations, dance and song
the natural and the grand
surprise of rainbows, birds and flowers
that shine throughout the land

beauty lies beneath the flow
of countless smiles and tears
commanding me and making me
its servant through the years...

by serving beauty I have learned
all life itself is served
hope and wisdom joy and love
are nobly preserved

when hearts are opened, truth will rise
and character will flower
as poets sing and celebrate
infused with beauty's power

in search of my muse

amid the quiet
I wondered which is worse
a plate so empty
there is no food for thought

or bowls awash
with poison
poured upon a nation
already in pain

inundating the compassionate
the creative minds
with pleas for wisdom
beyond human gift

the answer
is soaked in tears
and some days
the poet is silent

SIMPLE PLEASURES

Simple Pleasures
Words of inspiration in the *Daily Compass* told of the happiness of penguins with nothing more than sand, sea and sky to provide their comfort. It told of their acceptance of a single stone as a precious gift. "What small thing," the writers ask, "has made you happy?"

And I am perplexed, as my world is filled with small happy things that seem to me immense. I am comforted and entertained by three small dogs, gentled by leaves of green in patio containers and indoor pots. I am serenaded by the whirring of a tower fan, and jostled with laughter at a friend's internet posting. I am gifted with beauty as I gaze at photos on the bureau, framed drawings and paintings on the wall, created by my gifted family. I am reminded of the love that surrounds me as I giggle with my daughters during a brief chat or banter happily in "instant messages" between my son and me.

I am thankful today for fingers that move on the keyboard, for eyes that feast on beauty and read for information or for fun. I am grateful for the "glamorous walking stick" that made me a bit more safe and secure on city sidewalks, and for all the smiling people on my path reflecting back the smiles I send their way. I give thanks for all who read my words and all who encourage me to continue. I acknowledge joy!

Apple

Great mouthfuls of juicy, crispy apple reassure me of my healthy choice of nourishment. Tiny meatballs with their accompanying richness of onion and bell pepper had snuggled into a buttered bagel and fulfilled my needs for a hearty main dish. The apple came later.

And for some unknown reason I was moved to write about that apple, to record that moment of sweetness and snap. I left the paragraph to ripen, tossed it on the desktop and forgot about it.

Next morning when I noted the file labeled "apple" I assumed at first that I had recorded some necessary information for my computer care and support. Much to my delight I recovered instead a memory of a quiet meal and a potential gift.

What is the gift heralded by that crispy apple? What is the lesson of the "lake-house meatball" sandwich with its energizing protein and tasty veggies? Perhaps it is all about the noted sweetness and snap.

By being consciously aware of the varied flavors, the nourishing quality of that little meal I have enriched my life with pleasure and gratitude. I have gained another image of natural beauty and abundance. I have been permitted to write of joy and to share delight. Being in the moment and writing from an awareness of life's simple pleasures grants a blessing to us all.

That fondly remembered day happened to be Halloween, so I went on to embrace a different vegetable, the mighty pumpkin. Choosing my one and only orange dress, a soft green shrug to represent the vine, and my *"Perfect Pumpkin"* beret, I sallied forth to elicit smiles in the local supermarket, where shoppers were surprised by a "little old lady", crisp as an apple, pretending to be a pumpkin.

Good!

Oh, that was good!
I always say
expressing my joy
in a simple way
and my gratitude
for life's generous gift
for beauty and bounty
that gives me a lift
so often repeated
it's almost ignored
this phrase of contentment
acclaims life's reward

I listen to my inner response to life— my intimate reaction to whatever is happening or whatever life is gifting me. Do I hear myself praising or thanking the cosmos or perhaps even condemning it?

I've discovered that my automatic comment on the food I eat, the pleasant surprises life presents me, is always the same; *"Oh, that was good!"* No matter how modest the inspiration, it's always the same—umm, that was good!

The potatoes with onions and celery may be very ordinary, but hallelujah, they are tasty. The change from a sip of dry red wine to the delight offered by a little added honey syrup may be expected, but it carries a gift of goodness worthy of comment.

"Oh, that's good!" The words are a gift to myself as I recognize life's goodness and express my infinite gratitude. A simple expression of thankfulness so ingrained it has become a part of me. May it be the same for all of us! So much in life is good.

The Great Pumpkin

Charles Schultz's articulate young scholar, Linus, has always been a treasure trove of obscure and esoteric information. Because of this I have classified him in my mind as highly intelligent. But Linus, like the rest of us, has his weaknesses. He is first and foremost a blanket lover, and he is also a true believer.

Year after year we fans of the Peanuts gang have watched with Linus in a dark field of pumpkins on Halloween night. We were waiting with him for the appearance of *The Great Pumpkin*, an event Linus knew would surely come to pass. And every year he and we were once again disappointed, with a sadness greater than it needed to be.

Linus was so intently concentrating on the anticipated arrival that he neglected or failed to even see the abundance of regular ordinary pumpkins surrounding him in that patch. Perhaps he was the victim of orthodoxy or maybe he needed to prove to the world that his hero exists. Surely he stood firmly on his faith, to the point of blindness. My heart reaches out to that brave little boy.

The results of such single-mindedness are not enriching, however. If we are totally focused on a big win, a huge success, an earth-shaking event, we will miss the small treasures, the quiet accomplishments, the simple pleasures and sweet surprises that fill the spaces left by absence of the spectacular. If we demand to see and touch and prove the reality of the Great Pumpkin in our little patch, we may miss the pumpkin pies our Grandma left on the kitchen table.

Look at those ordinary and extraordinary pumpkins all around us, the miracles of everyday living—plain food, good folks, small gifts, songs sung, something accomplished, something learned. Come on, Linus, let's have a deep literary conversation or celebrate with Schroeder... Beethoven's birthday!

beautiful

my heart sings a single word
   beautiful
tall trees dance to that sweet song
   beautiful
shamrocks bloom in white and gold
wine and green adorn the lawn
   beautiful
wind chimes add their harmonies
birds make rollicking symphonies
with darting flights that need no tune
to bring a smile to earth's profile
   it's beautiful

Red, the Breadman

Once there were milkmen. These were the heroes who delivered beautiful cream-topped glass bottles of the precious liquid to our door at Road's End when I was a child. I don't remember what else might have been tucked away in Mr. Milkman's white truck, though I suspect there was butter and cream and perhaps cottage cheese to be had. And what a help to my overworked mother, having these necessaries delivered.

Milkmen, yes—but did you know there were also breadmen? In those early years, several bakery trucks plied their wares along country roads to deliver soft white loaves of Bond bread, rolls, buns, and coffee cakes, and who knows what all else. Hurrah for the breadmen!

One fellow in particular captured the heart of a merry curly headed blonde child named Taffy, as she had captured his. On his long treks along township gravel roads, the freckle faced young redheaded driver befriended his customers and looked forward to seeing the happy little cutie at the end of the road. He enjoyed his job. And Christmas was coming.

The papers were full of holiday ads...overrun with images of good Saint Nick. Red knew little Taffy would be waiting to greet him and would be happy for his visit. So he budgeted an extra fifteen minutes for the stop at Road's End all through the advent season. Fifteen minutes to get down on the floor with the newspapers and the child, racing to see who found the most Santa Claus pictures, and who saw them first. Of course he let the little girl win.

And so today a silver haired grandmother sits cozily writing and smiling at memories of kindnesses unheralded but deeply valued long ago and here in the distant present.

MINISTRY

Inspiriting

inspire me, require me
to lift spirit, lift my mind
talk with me, walk with me
we have miracles to find.

step softly, step lightly
let our lives become a dance
smile sweetly, discreetly
give our finest selves a chance.

shed sorrow, don't borrow
troubles that may never be.
give madly, help gladly
share the love with all we see.

grow stronger, laugh longer
find a way to give a lift
to the stranger in danger.
kindness is our greatest gift.

Intro-Extrovert

Consider the labels **introvert and extrovert**—either/or. Throughout the years I named myself extrovert. After all, I was the public face of the Unitarian Universalist congregation in our town, their preacher, their P.R. person, their "fearless leader." I stood before them to officiate at weddings and gifted them with compassion and comfort at funerals. It was my calling to speak and write the good word to all and sundry, letting my smile shine forth to the community at large. What could be more extroverted than that?

When taking 1980s Myers-Briggs tests I metaphorically shouted ENFP, answering as a classic extrovert, and certain this was the logical combination for our life-affirming clergy. I was, remember, not afraid of public speaking nor of caring for both friends and strangers. I little noted the disparity of being hyphenated by my beloved others and colleagues as poet-minister. Nor did I think about the usual image of writers and poets as solitary souls.

Today I look upon the postings of revered colleagues and see Ken or Paul and others naming themselves introvert with the same assurance I once had in an extroverted state. And I look upon my quiet life, retired, writing, caring for my doggy companions, and contented here. I can sit before the picture window and silently contemplate life's gifts or sally forth to smile and greet all who pass in the grocery store. I can chat with a visitor and give thanks for both their visit and their quick departure. I am neither extrovert nor introvert; and I am both.

In the Presence of Greatness

My heroes are not always recognized by everyone—as may be true for you, my friend. Perhaps you honor your uncle or sister, your teacher from third grade, or a drama coach who taught you how to command the stage and be a presence. Someone who opened the world for you by showing you how powerful you are and how great you can be.

My most widely known, honored, and beloved icon is the magnificent Maya Angelou. No explanation is needed. I am a poet, a minister, an activist for social justice, and one who honors wisdom and the truth of sacred oneness. *(..for we are more alike, my friend, than we are unalike)*. It is almost a forgone conclusion that I would be a disciple of mother Maya.

Perhaps less known to the wider community, another of my true heroes and mentors, my west coast father figure and minister or chaplain is– was the late great Stephen H. Fritchman. I have always treasured the gift of his care and blessed the fates that allowed me to be a surrogate daughter to him and my children to meet him. My daughter Kristi shared his birthday and I was the fortunate recipient of his thoughtful and loving little hand-written notes.

The Rev Dr. Fritchman delivered the charge to the minster at my ordination-installation in 1973. The instruction he gave was that I should be "...a pioneer of a new age, a minister to the people, a woman (in a time when so few among the clergy were women), a friend, a prophet, a poet, a priest." He used the concept of prophecy, not as foretelling, but as telling forth that which needs to be spoken—speaking my truth. He set me free to be all that I could be. He blessed me.

I honor the memory of Steven Fritchman with deepest respect and love, and give thanks to have been, so early in my ministry, nurtured in the presence of greatness.

Charge to the Minister
When one of our congregations ordains or installs a new minister, the ceremony includes exhortations and bits of wisdom, indicating what the duties, the needs, and the gifts of grace may be for each, and these words are called the Charge to the Minister and the Charge to the Congregation.

beyond the pulpit

much changes, life engulfs me, I grow old
my body may refuse to bear its load
yet I am ever who I've always been
with a prophetic story to unfold.

poet, prophet, priest, he labeled me
teller of truths that can't be left unsung
a holy woman, sister, soldier, sage.
be brave, he said, when you're no longer young.

let your words, your stories ease the minds
of needful, hopeful folks alone and lost
feeling dismayed, believing they've no power.
teach them that finding peace is worth its cost.

the simple gift of quiet, splendid truth
is bought with thoughts of goodness—with a smile
and kindness, for the world is hard and grim.
tell of this truth, this wisdom most worthwhile.

and so I must continue, write, and teach
sharing a tale more vital than is known
with lessons bringing comfort, beauty, love
to myriad souls who'll learn they're not alone.

Listening

To be a counselor, guru or coach one must first of all be a listener.

Loquacious speechmakers calling themselves teachers or guides have missed the basic truth that teaching happens only when learning takes place. And usually the learning begins with a listening teacher. This subject seems to demand wonderful quotations from Gibran or Spinoza but footnotes and authority are not what my writings are built upon. My study is a corner for contemplation, a place for pondering. . .

I have never been called taciturn, curt or laconic. Yet my gift of presence has always been about listening. Pastoral care, parenting, and the wisdom of the crone or shaman all rest on the peaceful, mindful strength of the non-anxious listener. Few words are needed when you are secure in the reality that your story is being intently noted. Sometimes the solution to a problem presents itself in the very telling, when a calm, interested audience offers the support of a willing ear.

To follow the path of my thought, I began this reflection wondering about pleasant silences and reminding myself that I am most useful when I am a good listener. For years I have made a joke to the effect that I must wear a sign somewhere upon my person that reads, "Chaplain - tell me your story." Not all of those looking to use my sounding board are looking for spiritual guidance or comfort however. Some want to tap the wordsmith's treasure store of language or the poet's melodic awareness. Some even want to share a moment's delight. And so I listen.

The story of reading #653 in the *Unitarian Universalist LIVING TRADITION* hymnal

The year was 1973 and we were in the midst of a fuel shortage. The people of the Bangor Unitarian congregation were frightened and depressed, fearing the winter's depravations and believing even Christmas would mean nothing to them. As their pastor it was my mandate to bring them comfort. This was my gift to my beloved people—

Reflections on the Resurgence of Joy

How short the daylight hours have now become.
How gray the skies; how barren seem the trees.
A damp and chilling wind has gript my mind,
    and made me gloomy, too.
But look, now, past December's leafless trees,
And see the opal glow on purple hills we couldn't see in June.
The view at last is open to our sight,
And we see wonders hid before.
A silver lake lies there beyond the wood;
I never knew that it was there—'til now.
I walk down Main Street,
Past the tinsel gleam of storefront Christmas,
And I hear— a tune— familiar, yes
And joyful, too; from years when I was small,
Was young and eager and convinced.
There's more to my inheritance
Than Puritan New England's mincemeat pie—
There's joy! It comes in contrast to

The day's bleak rain, the night's long lonely waiting.
It comes in the folkways and music of Christmas.
Now here's the time for a party!
Oh, I'm not Pollyanna-sure that sadness isn't real.
I know it's real, and I have known it's bite.
Indeed without the salt of many tears
I could not taste the sweet of candy canes.
But there is that in me which reaches up into the light,
And laughs with laughter, sings along with bells and carolers.
I know in my deepest knowing
That my religious myth of reborn joy
And goodness in relationship is true.
It carries with it all the truths of older myths—
That light returns and conquers darkness,
That life surges in the evergreen...and us
Tho winter storms may come,
That babes are hope, and saviors of the world
And miracles abound in common things.
I hear you, sayers of doom;
I weigh you words, your forecasts of disaster;
And I reach out my hand in fellowship
To beckon you on, beyond your gloom— into discovery.
Good things are bound to happen;
New values are emerging in the land,
And this present valley is the place
From whence we see the mountain peak.
Praise be that life's not flat!
How could we know a moment's ecstasy
Without joy's ebb and flow? Rejoice!
And join in the gladness of Christmas.

Papa's wildflower garden...No need for drama.

Life Lessons - Learned from Papa

Proverbs 15:1
A soft answer turneth away wrath.

"I'm not mad at you, Babe." Such a small, intimate saying, spoken often by a gentle, peace-loving man to his passionate wife. Such a powerful determinant in the making of a minister.

Over a lifetime of teaching, I have spent more than fifty years guiding others to kindness and peaceful behavior using the written and spoken word—writing and preaching. I did not learn this technique at seminary nor from books or classes offered across the continent. I learned to deliver joy from my beautiful father.

Papa smiled. He sang. He danced with his wife and his daughters at the small town charity balls. He hugged us and cherished us, protected us, and encouraged us.

And when my mother's anger arose, he would simply say, "I'm not mad at you, Babe." No anger in return. No need for drama.

And I LEARNED.

Funny, the caps appeared without any help from me.

I'm not mad at you, Babe. It taught me how to be mellow, how to raise my children, how to educate the world with my Daddy's kindness. Charles Arthur Isaksen— wise man for the ages— thank you.

Let this be my prayer.

Spirit of Life—
Help me to fill my little bucket
with the strength I need
to be compassionate and kind
and the wisdom to give respect,
to give thanks,
to give forgiveness.
Keep me mindful
of the sacredness
of this very present moment
and centered herein.
Attune me to the tranquility
that rests within me
and the enthusiasm
that can light the universe.
Teach me to carry the light
and spread it
that it may
overcome darkness
and to look always for the best.
Open my eyes and ears
to beauty everywhere
and ignite the fires of creativity
that my small gifts might serve others.
Give me the courage
to spread joy
and teach only love.
Amen

Creative Mistakes

Make grand and glorious mistakes, a guru advises, and I smile at the wisdom urging creative error. My mistakes may not have been grand or glorious, but they were mine and I wore them humbly and honestly.

I have admitted from the pulpit that I recognized the call to be a role model which accompanied the call to ministry. I knew that the best I had to offer as a role model however, was deeply flawed and utterly human. I certainly couldn't model perfection, nor even some earthly ideal, but I could and did model human frailty. I erred. I missed the mark. I sometimes failed in my endeavors.

Sometimes, like all of us, I got it right...

When I messed up, however, I chose to model self-forgiveness. I chose to open myself to the lesson an error might have brought. This was my gift to a congregation wanting redemption. I showed them error is forgivable and human imperfection is normal, beautiful, and just fine.

To do my best and live as if that is enough—is enough. And to show up, keep up the good work, make the effort, to discover something new, smile and spread joy, and to love—this is what is required of me, of us all. This was the opportunity open to my beloveds as they stumbled along beside me. We could make our mistakes boldly!

AGING

Age sweetly

Age Sweetly

Age is so much more than a number. It is an attitude, an inheritance, a promise. If you are bright-eyed and interested in others, eager, enthusiastic and humorous, you will glow with the same energy and delight as any youngster, whatever your years may number. If, however, you are grim and disinterested, self-absorbed and negative you have already lost any youth with which your numbered years may have gifted you.

A sweet disposition can last a lifetime, maturing the kind, merry youngster into a sweet, kind, and merry sage. It is never too late to be young.

After the Fall

Late on a Saturday night I fell and was unable to save myself. The Life Alert theme of "I've fallen and I can't get up" which has become both an advertising catchword and a cruel joke, is all too true. Once down, an arthritic elder cannot find a way to regain her stability. Feet slip, knees refuse to hold, only the combined support of two strong rescuers can raise this fallen senior, and the experience is exceedingly frightening and traumatizing.

After the fall I managed to stop shaking, but was left with tension and suspicious aches and pains in arms and legs, in my chest and my neck, along with a need to sleep, and a desire for a soothing latte. I told myself, "Tomorrow will be better." It was.

Flying

I didn't take flying lessons, nor even write about them on a bucket list, but I have flown. Unintentionally, of course, and without license, but... That *trip-over-a-hassock-in-the-dark* at our former home had me airborne indeed, and the latest crash involved a short flight as well. As has been said many times, it is not the flying nor the falling that is the problem; it is the landing.

Much to my good fortune, my landing on Thursday (at least that of my face) was buffered by the padded arms of a recliner, and my unscheduled flying lesson was short and simple. I shall remain earthbound and be sure to move with care.

Once again flying without a license

I did it again,
much to my regret
I flew.
election day...6/5/18, found me damaged,
betrayed by a new pair of shoes.

pretty though they were
those sandals...just a wee bit too large
caught on the carpet and threw me
airborne
against the wall.

ouch

I have been called bionic
with titanium joints in place,
two hips and one old shoulder
assembled through the years.
the shoulder complains
this roughhouse flight
must cease.
ankles, knees, and elbows
all agree.

falling
is marketed as comedy.
it is not funny.
for those who are
breakable, the drama
is measured in pain.
if I have a choice
I prefer not to be
a fearless flyer.

Fractured

OK, so I'm known for my positive approach to life. Sue me. I'm guilty. Today I may have won an award or made a record. My daughter certainly laughed a lot when I announced that my leg x-ray showed a fracture and followed that announcement with expressions of delight. (It is not a clot.) This she said, had to be an outstanding example of positive spin.

Rewind.

The medical examination scheduled to investigate the pain that had made walking excruciating for a week sent me to the imaging center for both x-ray and ultrasound. The physician's assistant who was assigned to me had an immediate concern about a blood clot possibly causing the pain. Thus the ultra sound. And that caused a deep concern. Blood clots can wander. Wandering hematoma may lodge in the heart or the brain. and that, my friend, is terrifying.

So I am joyful, I am thankful, I am filled with peace and wonder. My years do not weigh heavily but sing with enthusiasm and hopefulness. Today is good. And so is every day that greets me with the rising of the sun. I may house a little fracture, but I am not broken!

Ephemeral

Never knowing what tomorrow may bring, I choose to live as if there is only today.
>   Only today in which I can be grateful,
>   Only today to share a poem,
>   Only today to say I love you,
>   Only today to do and dream.

Love, I'm sure, is forever. Love with a capital L is the stuff of which we're made, the eternal soul of you or me that will last beyond death to warm hearts in memory. But the love which is simple appreciation and admiration lasts only for those moments when we awaken to its call.

When asked to name some of the books that had brought change into my life, I thought of The *Little Prince* by St. Exupery. The Prince learned that his beloved Rose was *ephemeral*, which is to say in danger of speedy disappearance. And so are we all—and much that we love—in danger of speedy disappearance. Only the truth of love-in-action will preserve life's ephemera in life's memory. And so I treasure the gifts of my life, express my gratitude and activate my recognition and kindness.

Pretty Feet

Once upon a time, long ago, indeed—bright smile and blue-green eyes not withstanding—my friends and I made jokes about the gorgeousness of (get this!) my feet. It's true; my feet were beautiful.

Not that it mattered. I was not entering the modeling profession to display expensive footwear, nor looking for an admirer with a foot fetish. My little feet were simply the dainty denizens of my little shoes—the useful tools of my coming and going, the promise of my dancing.

In those days of hot-tub entertainments and backyard weddings, I laughed with my dear ones at the ridiculousness of this small attraction of mine, even without knowing quite how ephemeral it was. And then came the arthritis.

First appeared a hammertoe on the right foot. Not even dignified by a serious medical name, a middle toe jumped out of alignment and stuck its knuckle high above the graceful lineup of perfect digits. And the years marched on bringing ever more arthritis.

Hammertoes soon joined the chorus line on the left foot as well and eventually the disquieting twistedness of the disease crept upon the lesser toes and tilted the whole left foot beyond fitting—the little toe could not be completely tucked into my shoe. Shoes that accommodate my feet became ever more difficult to find, and ever less attractive.

Sometime during this odyssey an ingrown toenail made itself known and brought with it an infection that required the total and permanent removal of the nail on my big toe. I am left with a weird and ugly lump of tissue and an alligator-skin toe tip. No pretty polished toenails for this girl!

And so the beauty of my feet, so amusing to the young persons in this story, has languished and died, leaving in its place the beauty of a creative mind and a merry sense of humor, and that is enough.

from New Year 2015
to a joyous year
every day a new beginning
every hour a new delight
let your heart be full of singing...
dancing brighten up your night

looking back and looking forward
years before us, moments past
filled with images of growing,
learning, giving, love to last

memories to share and treasure
some to honor and let go
simply must we seek the lesson
or the gift we've come to know

every day a new beginning
every life part of 'the one'
as we share the blessed journey
thankful for the course we've run

Snow-topped Mountains

There is a special delight in living within sight of the mountains.
Just north of us lie the San Gabriels, crowned by Mt. San Antonio
(affectionately known as Mt. Baldy). Various local communities claim
the right to name their highways and byways *Mountain*, be it Mountain
Street, Avenue, or Boulevard—much to the confusion of travelers new
to Southern California.

Our mountains in this drought-plagued landscape, denied the green
of eastern hills, rise in awesome grayness sometimes hidden by mists
of smog or clouds that refuse to give up their life giving rain. Still the
sight of them blesses us and makes us smile. The arrival of snow, when
it finally appears on the rocky peaks leaves us giddy with delight.

What is it about snow on the mountains that so easily pleases? And why do we fragile humans balk at the first sign of white on our own summits? Perhaps we need to recognize the beauty in silver strands among our darker locks, indicating that we, too, stand firm in our chosen lives, learning some small truths from the mighty hills as the seasons change.

Tired—so tired. . .

and yet. . .
I wonder, ponder, analyze–
What was it like when those more wise
found simple pleasures with much less—
enough to please and to possess.

Why yearn for tools to serve a need
that won't exist if we succeed
in simplifying life itself
and putting greed upon the shelf.

Perhaps the folks in cabins small
were not so tired after all.
Theirs the quiet peaceful days
with restful nights and words of praise.

With children, teens and twenties sad
and weary from a life that's mad
from struggle and from hours too long
we need a simpler wiser song.

I don't think I intended to write a poem as I opened myself to thoughts of the weariness that seems to overcome almost everyone, and my seeming so much more tired than I was when young. But I have learned the years are not to blame. My children and grandchildren and the great grandchildren of my friends suffer too, from this eternal exhaustion. It appears to be endemic. We expect too much of ourselves and make small tasks into large projects just because we can. This is my call for rest and rehabilitation for peace and quiet. Breathe. Smile. Refresh. Renew.

Upon contemplating the young woman I once was.
How sad we never know how lovely we all are.
The mirror doesn't tell us what we need to know, and
Each new look, dress size, hair style just brings a change
But never opens up the truth of thee and me
Or how we face the world and how it sees us.

Until the years have torn away our charms
And camouflaged our gifts with flesh or wrinkles.
And only character remains to soften crooked teeth
Or double chins, arthritic fingers, feet and knees—
And open up our eyes to beauty once unseen
When we were young and oh so unaware.

Pure Delight

imagine, if you will
a woman seated, quiet, still,
her image in precisely
distanced mirror

from here she sees her hair
gleaming silver, visage fair
all that classic ancient sweetness
seems to cheer her

then with trust she asks for truth
knowing nothing measures youth
her facade was built
and sculptured far too long

Now she is a work of art
and her mischief has a part
to play if we but listen
to her song

as she looks upon that face
so well molded by her grace
she recalls the girl who was,
the elf who lives...

she begins to laugh with joy
at a life time can't destroy
and shares the pure delight
that aging gives.

it's all about the hair

silver halo, waves or curls
its all about the hair
crone or purple velvet queen
    its all about the hair

her morning face may sparkle
and greet her with a grin
or simply manage not to spoil
the day now to begin
    its all about the hair

you might admire her teal blue eyes
with merriment they dance
appreciate the friendly smile
and poems that entrance
    it's still about the hair

the mirror tells a story
sings each day a different song
declaring "pretty woman" or
today you look all wrong
    it's all about the hair

photographers make art of her
show charm in growing old
rejoicing in the gift of truths
their pictures will unfold
    (it's all about the hair!)

How to Be a Badass Matriarch

First of all, outlast the family founders,
Live long and prosper as Spock would say.
Octogenarian, faith Unitarian
Gives an advantage in most every way.

Welcome the far-flung relations and feed them.
With social media keep all in touch.
Write books and blogs full of militant positives
Knowing the world needs your wisdom so much.

Elegant, tasteful, both sassy and classy,
Co-ordinated from earring to shoe,
Day to day wear looking all put together
A ladylike class act. It's just what we do

Be the best listener (no interruptions)
Demand a "Sing to me" of scamming thugs.
Non-judging sounding board, totally present
Comforting anyone with smiles and hugs.

Greet scowling shoppers with small rays of sunshine.
Wear your adorable orange beret
Complete the look with a glamorous walking stick
Or Danish walker for safety—hooray!

Dignified even when reading rude sayings
Against humankind, it's only a game.
Learn well the eye roll to share with the grown-ups
Flow with the tide, there is no one to blame.

Forego old limited binary thinking,
Welcome diversity, courage to be. . .
Rescue a floundering program or service
With powerful presence and fine poetry.

COMPANIONS

**you walked with me
(on meeting Mary)**

your smile
your gift of friendship
made me stronger

no special words
were needed
no supporting arm

though 't might
have helped one
differently abled

you walked with me

the distance
seemed less long
the pain less pressing

when we were one
in such a simple way

because
with tender heart
you chose—
to greet me

and

to walk with me.

Mirror

Beauty shines forth from her face
Dignity and strength are there
Eyes that sparkle blue or green
Waves of silver in her hair

Beauty earned through many years
Never noted never sung
By her mother, or her mate
In the days when she was young.

But now she sings...
surprised am I...
the mirror smiles
it does not lie.
What long ago
I dared not see
and thought
that I had not been told
Was said by friends
who spoke my worth
by them whose friendship
shines like gold

I remember...

The friend who told forth my courage,
announced my beauty to the world
and praised always the songs of my soul
and the workings of my muse.

And he who named me "Gorgeous"
celebrated my mind, tended my spirit
and nurtured my growing wisdom.

with belated thanks dear friends
12/25/13

Canine Companions

Some would say I live alone
no longer chatelaine nor wife
nor guardian, pastor, family chef
yet three small dogs enhance my life.

Three dogs—
companions, merry friends
sharing my cottage small
fur-babies quickstep 'round the room
I am not lonely here at all

Toto growls and scampers
tossing kibbles round the floor
he doesn't beg his ball be tossed
but plays alone and dances more
pretending that he's vicious
fierce and tough with his attack
creating playthings for himself
chasing his toys across and back

Monkey poses prettily
with eyes adoring, sweet
he wants to tell us he's so cute

and needs a special treat
he's quick to sit beside *Maman*
if Toto is too slow
and sings his stories, tells his tales
saying "I love you so."

Stevie, street-wise rescue pup
a beautiful brown and black
all silky ears and melting gaze
that begs for love and gives it back
builder of blanket forts and beds
tongued vacuum cleaner of the floor
this little one is alpha dog
over the dinner bowls and more.

Toto...telling me to follow him.

Talk with the Animals

One morning I was caressing Toto, and noticed what felt like crusted blood on his throat. Upon checking, I was surprised to discover a raw spot on his neck, with a clump of hair torn from beneath his chin. It didn't cause him to complain when I touched it, so I thankfully decided he was not severely damaged.

A little later, I opened the sliding doors for the thundering herd made up of the three small yappy dogs, and the first two dashed out as always. Toto, however, sat just outside the door, refusing to go further, telling me to follow him. . .

He stepped onto the patio then sat and stared at me. I asked him what he wanted and he took a few steps, then stopped to stare at me once again. I walked out onto the patio and Toto ran a short distance and stopped to give his "Come on, Mom" look. He took me to the side of the paved yard near the gate, but try as I might, I couldn't discover what he wanted to show me.

Giving Toto's problem further thought, and noting his disinterest in going outdoors that morning, I believe he may have had an unfortunate encounter with the local possum, and is fearful as a result. This would explain his stay-abed attitude when he clearly wasn't in pain or ill.

Opossum
Our nocturnal visitor set off the doggy alarm at about four one morning. Monkey went into high alert and screamed in the voice of panic and the others added their loudest warnings until I had left my bed, turned on lights in the cottage and the yard, and opened the door for the three to exit.

The dogs galloped out to surround a hungry opossum hiding behind the dog food bin, while shouting their disapproval. They chose, however, to return to their beds at Mother's call. No need to challenge those sharp 'possum teeth, after all, with the bin sealed shut and their kibble safe from uninvited diners.

My small furry companion warms my knees and rests his head on the arm of my chair, reminding me, as is his mission in life, that God is love— unending, unchanging, unconditional love. Thus sings my Universalist soul.

Finches
(a song of freedom)

the birds measure but a few inches
the sweet rosey-breasted house finches
that frequent the tree by my window
and feast on the seed waiting there

some splash in the bath or the fountain
happy here at the foot of the mountain
bringing with them an image of freedom
and delight in the garden we share

though I've watched birds on branches for ages
I can't bear to see them in cages
wanting always to share with them
vistas of vast open space

the mocking bird, dove, and the jay here
unfettered and free, choose to stay here
winging dances of rich classic beauty airborne
gifting us all with their grace

The Mexican Woman
For Elizabeth

when left to my own devices
I find myself sometimes in crisis
needing a helper, a caregiver
here by my side...
a strong knowing woman
who shows skill
whenever it's needed.
she just will
use a skrewdriver,
brush, or the needle
that she is prepared to provide.

my little home sparkles
with neatness
the pantry is filled
in completeness
dogs clean and content
garden watered and trimmed
I am blessed.
at the store, car repair or the Xray
my stolid companion
will just stay
by my side keeping me
safe and smiling.
she knows that quiet is best.
she solves, she repairs,
making fears cease
building beauty and order
that brings peace.
her powers are born
of her fearless and creative gift.
nothing can frighten or beat her
you'll know this as soon
as you meet her...
this mother, this daughter,
this woman who gives life a lift

SNIPPETS

**No thought is too small. No one is beneath notice.
All are worthy.**

Snippets

. . .and what of the little snippets of thought that light a writer's mind and reach for their place among the annals of her creativity? Do they molder and disappear because they are insufficient to fill the space allotted for today's work? Do they remain unspoken or unwritten when they make no claim on the topic of the day? Or do we intrepid poets and journalists, drop them quietly all alone somewhere or tuck them away, hidden amid the brilliance of a longer piece?

Yet again, that little thought might provoke deeper consideration and outgrow its snippet brevity to achieve daily topic status. Let thoughts not be lost, poet, make them shed their light. Here's a puzzle for the mind, much like the old saw, "Why did the chicken cross the road?" This little notion floats through the ether of my consciousness. Why did this question cross my mind? What do I need to learn today? How will I grow? What of this shall I give to the world?

First I must discover some truth for myself. I believe it is this: *No thought is too small. No one is beneath notice.* All are worthy.

Nettles

Berries on a bramble bush are clearly sending a message—pay attention! Look for the gift carried inside the pain, the lesson held within the stickered branches. I have sometimes been blessed with these gifts and understandings, much to my own surprise, unwilling though I may be..

Lesser annoyances might be thought of as nettles—prickling stinging and sending their jolts of discomfort without the warning posted in the bramble bush. Without the sweet succulent taste of the berry, either. This tends to make us cranky.

And so I offer a small suggestion—be kind to yourself. If you're weary, hurting, bored or yes, cranky, do something nice for yourself or for someone you love. Buy a posy, write a note, make a phone call, take a stroll, pet the pup.

You deserve delight and so does that someone who is important to you. Just for being you and just for being a person. As Horton tells us...no matter how small, a person's a person after all. Splurge a little. It works for me.

Lament for October in California

October, most beloved of all
the months when there was truly Fall.
New England's crisp and spicy breeze
and heaven's paint brush in the trees
made me rejoice with gratitude
and share my Autumn attitude,
my love for this so precious time.
now I've but sun and tropic clime
alas, there is no Autumn here
October never comes I fear.

The Quilt

quilting
like a metaphor for life
brings scraps together
in a work of art.
stitch and patch
arrange and match
the whole more beautiful
than any part.

a square of denim
diamond of pure white
a piece of shirting
plaid with colors bright
the pocket of an apron
soft and old
a bit of flowered dress
more pale than bold.

is this a pile of rags
a tangled mess?
or truth and beauty
sent our lives to bless

the artist crafts
a picture, a design
made up of many parts
all rich and fine.

each piece is precious
each unique and sweet
the varied patterns
like earth's children meet,
each one enriching others
in god's quilt
with gifts of joy and peace
on which it's built.

WORDS

My Life's an Epic Poem

Justin is my eldest Grand. He is an actor, and he sings—almost constantly at home, in the car, wherever—with a sweetness of voice envied by the angels. And I dare to complain. I want more, and the songs are sometimes too soft for these old ears. I hate to miss a single note or lyric. Since he was a tad in elementary school, Justin's life has been a Broadway musical.

Mine is an epic poem.

With no gift for singing or playing a musical instrument, my melodies explode into all I write or share as the spoken word. As a Wordsmith-poet, my uninhibited public displays of affection for my beloved "WORDS" announce this lifelong love affair.

In the beginning was the word
and the word was beloved. .

romancing the words

wordlove held me in its sheltering song
from childhood keeping me verbally strong
blessing the words

the language I love brightly bloomed on the page
teaching me, reaching me from book or stage
caressing the words

preaching or writing, my ardor is spoken
through four generations my passion unbroken
romancing the words

in essay or poem the thoughts I invited
then crafted and polished. the fire ignited
dancing the words

this gift so primordial guided my living
molded me making me loving and giving
dancing, romancing and singing
I'm waltzing the words

*I looked up the word for the study of bugs and found entomology. I suppose I
thought having this word in my wordsmith's pouch might help me write about
the poor lost grub climbing up my windowpane. But it's 7:15 at night, and
the temperature is 99—I'm not cool enough just now to celebrate an insect...*

tell her

the poet's words
wear passion's fire
to teach of life
and to inspire—
tell her

her beauty she'd
not recognize
her gifts may come
as a surprise—
tell her

tho she is young
and ego free
she soon must learn
what she will be—
tell her

in years when
she's grown old and wise
applaud the sparkle
in her eyes,
although her feet
no longer dance
your truths will
honor and entrance—
tell her

Picture Books

What a sad and lonely house it must be that has no wealth of children's books. My own babes were surrounded with stories and poems, warm laps to snuggle on, cozy corners to hide in with their favorite few. A. A. Milne's collected treasures kept company with the big blue book of children's classics. *To Think That it Happened on Mulberry Street,* and *Are You My Mother?* regaled the adult readers along with the listening tots.

When the grandchildren came, a toddler library claimed the heart of this minister's study and I became enraptured with picture books—sharing adventures with *Good Dog Carl,* whispers in *The Napping House,* and giggles awaiting *The Big Hungry Bear.* To add to all that joy, I discovered Mark Buehner's exquisite heart-warming and witty illustrations.

Absolutely anything illustrated by the gifted Buehner would be a bargain at its price. His cloud-babies, cumulous cows or elephants, and fluffy sky-sailing ships delight. His repeated, almost hidden kitty, pup or ostrich challenges and encourages the searching puzzle solver in all of us. His humorous depiction of the beauty found in the ordinary inspires. I found myself (a life-long wordsmith) choosing the books, not for the words, but for pictures worth so many. Yes, even Theodor Geisel's funny little mustachioed Lorax is worth at least a thousand words.

thinking about that word. . .
Et cetera

what is the meaning, in truth,
of this old word
et cetera
where is it leading us
why is it there
this et cetera

is it just sloth entitling an author
to name simple listings memory garners
and lazily crowns with the magical shortcut
et cetera

in business when someone has something to add,
it is then kind and useful to open the pathway
by gifting a colleague or friend with this doorway—
"et cetera"

does it perhaps urge the reader to ponder
to reach for the missing unlisted criteria
stretch the mind further to meet a new challenge
et cetera

or does it protect me, the writer, from needing
to act and respond with concern or solutions
to ease the world's anger, the greed, and the meanness
et cetera

if I choose and refuse to include in my listings
to simply ignore and not name hateful practices
sadly the unnamed drifts into oblivion
et cetera

Word Surprise

On a tall wooden stool, I perch like a bird, having seated my treasured guests in cushioned parson's chairs. My comfort is in their presence, their conversation, their smiles and laughter. I delight in every visit and savor the moments we are together.

When I am alone I hold inner conversations, ponder obscure questions, note interesting anomalies. And I read. Among my literary escapes and escapades, I find descriptions of Tudor or Elizabethan London, grim and *noisome*.

Now, really. Noisome? Wouldn't you associate such a word with the boom and rattle, the cacophony of this city in the late middle ages? Indeed. Yet the slippery little adjective is just telling us the place stinks. Who knew? Isn't language fun!

Candy Hearts

"Be mine," they said, those tiny candy hearts
my mother bought in bright red cardboard box.
Or "cutie pie," "my baby doll,"
"say yes," perhaps, or maybe, "come to me."

But always there were words
that said be mine.
and we were left
with nothing of ourselves,
should we decide
to follow where that leads.

Sweet Valentine,
I've listened, and I've learned,
and I have become—my very own.
Not hers nor his nor theirs but mine alone,
fulfilled and free to love all life can give.

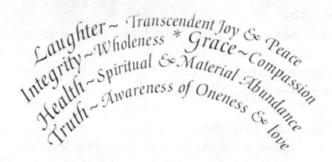

Words of L I G H T...

Words, Please

I'm longing for connection.
speak with me, I pray
in words, in language crisp and true
to make clear what you say

tell me—not in alphabets
in jargon, code or screen
use the real words, not to hide
but tell just what you mean

don't "LOL" me—say you have
a giggle or guffaw
a chuckle and a merry grin
and let me share your awe

words, these ordinary words
will carry truth and cheer
the beauty of your sparkling eyes
the laughter ringing clear

initialisms, acronyms
will leave me unaware
shut out by secret messages
you do not choose to share

still uninformed and unconnected
wanting to be friends
yet feeling robbed of precious words
until this madness ends

P O C

P O C—These, also, are initials used to replace a frequently used phrase. I choose to reinterpret and expand them, romancing the words to enhance the letters with grace and humanity. *P O C—Persons of color so are we all…*

I too, am a person of color
my complexion Nordic blonde,
my hair snowy with age,
my hands spotted brown
and gnarled with the labors of love
but I would be so much more than this

I would be
P O C—a person of courtesy
a person of civility and kindness

I must be
P O C—a person of conscience
ever caring, never cruel

I may be
P O C—a person of creativity, spreading joy
with my small hopeful gifts of poetry and prose

I will be
P O C—a person of credibility, trustworthy and true
a person of constancy and commitment,
someone to be depended upon

help me to be
P O C—a person of courage,
daring to speak truth to power
striving to protect the disinherited

I shall be
P O C—a person of compassion,
ever and always a person of love
and compassion
P O C—

We have forgotten what once we knew:
"We are one with the cosmos."

We yearn to touch,
to connect,
To reawaken our knowing
And re-member
our dismembered
Oneness.

CPSIA information can be obtained
at www.ICGtesting.com
Printed in the USA
BVHW030719071219
565856BV00013B/9/P